SOUL PATHWAY TO TOTAL HEALTH

It's no news to the common person that the mind and the body play a huge role in their relationship to each other to affect our overall health in general. This book sheds light on the role of our soul in our wellness (soul loss, spirit attachment and out of body experience), which is hugely underestimated in our physical, mental and spiritual health and well being. Writing this book was a cure for me as I have grown physically, mentally and spiritually healthier making my yes a yes and my no a no. If knowledge is power, understanding it must be a cure.

AHMED Y. TATIETA

ISBN 978-0-578-50375-2
Copyright 2016 Ahmed Tatieta.

SOUL PATHWAY TO TOTAL HEALTH

AHMED Y. TATIETA

For my family and children and everyone that believed in me.

Note from the Author: These writings were initially destined for my personal use. My goal was to glean more knowledge and gain further understanding so that I could answer questions that have arisen during my adult years, coupled with certain health issues I faced that I needed to address. The quest to find answers threw me into years of intensive research for more than five years. This process, and the knowledge I gained, appeased a crying spirit within me, a craving to know and understand what I was experiencing within my body.

After sharing my findings with friends and family, they urged me to compile what I'd learned into a book that would be helpful to the general public and perhaps assist others in resolving questions about their own health.

Caution is advised where personal views and experiences are expressed, as the information that follows has been filtered through my understanding so expressed. This book is not intended to induce or educate anyone and should only be used as you, the reader, deems it worthy for your personal needs and as you can relate to what is written.

Some of the descriptions involving health issues are not based on any scientific basis; the tone in some of the writing is rather centered more from a spiritual viewpoint and understanding.

In general, I believe the book will be interesting to and educational for everyone to some degree, regardless of one's social status, gender or race. It will raise awareness and the importance of self-control. It allows help in understanding human health without the use of medical terms or medical jargon, which is how I finally came to understand it.

This book highlights the importance of love, mutual respect, our responsibilities towards the universe, and the respect needed for other cultures and traditions, which can lead to greater tolerance and acceptance in peace, with neither prejudice nor discrimination. It embodies a hint of spirituality that can eventually contribute to awakening to the truth that encourages non-violence and law- abiding actions. Ultimately, this book may lead one to a state of self-realization.

ACKNOWLEDGEMENTS

Mr. and Mrs. Tatieta (dad and mom), Eric and Desire Scott.

TABLE OF CONTENTS

Introduction.. 1
What is perfect or total health? 2
The importance of energy in human life. 3
The sources of energy 5
What depletes the energy within the body?................. 7
Stress and its importance. 9
Holistic treatment versus allopathic treatment........ 11
The definition of soul loss 12
The meaning of spirit attachment 13
The origins of sickness and their symptoms............... 14
The relationship between the soul and the body including their shared symptoms 16
The relationship between the body and the soul....... 20
The realm of the living and the non-living................ 23
Laws of the universe applied to human bodily functions... 29
Unspoken laws determining our future physical health 39
The invisible wire and its relationship to the body.. 45
The relationship between the energy field, the mind and the body. 48
The aura 54
The importance of the aura in connection to the body.. 55

Relationship between the aura, the mind and the body to the universe. 57

The importance of cleansing the aura and its related symptoms. 60

Symptoms that prove you may have attachments on your aura and need cleansing. 62

Imperative rules of wellness 63

Karma: the supreme law. 67

The duality in the universe. 74

Human beings, owners of their destiny. 76

Understanding the world. 80

Universal relativity of our perceptions and actions. 83

Understanding yourself and people around you. 85

The universality of the truth 91

Quest for the truth and its difficulties. 95

Truth is only found by the strong-minded people. ... 99

Universal equality of mankind 102

Bibliography 105

INTRODUCTION

Mankind is not meant to fall sick. We were created so that we could be harmed by our own choices or by actions and events that occur in the universe. If we adopt a healthy, positive lifestyle, coupled with an understanding of the lessons offered by the universe, we can grow old without falling sick and without major health issues that might lead to premature death.

There is a right way to live and there is a wrong way to live. Getting sick is a reminder that our life is precious and should be lived with care and consideration. It's one way to remind us that our life is freely given; but, if we really want to live well, we must hold on to it by learning how to keep ourselves healthy. In educating ourselves on how to stay healthy, we become evermore curious about the universe and ourselves. I believe the whole purpose of our journey is to rediscover what we are made of and what the world around us is made of.

What is perfect or total health?

The human being is composed of a body, a mind, and a soul. The body, the mind and the soul are inseparable and interdependent. The imbalance of one affects the others and vice versa. For a person to be in perfect health physically, mentally and spiritually, the body, the mind and the soul must be in perfect balance. Therefore, in caring for one of the three, we should care for the other two as well, for all three (body, mind, soul) are joined in one. Another way to say this is that positive health – be it mental, physical or spiritual – depends upon three factors, which are interconnected. First, are the body's structural systems and their functions including the body's biochemical processes and the elimination of wastes. The second component is made up of the person's state of mind and emotions. The third factor merges the mind and emotions with the spiritual dimension of the person. When there is a balance between these three components, we have health. But when imbalances exist within any of these factors, or in their relationship with one another, illness occurs.

The importance of energy in human life.

Energy within the person binds the Body, the Mind and the Soul together and keeps them healthy and strong. Energy is the ability to do work. In terms of the human body, work allows the continuation of cellular and human life. The body needs energy in order for its organs to fully function normally. Energy is the body's vital force that moves the blood that nourishes the body's organs in order to produce **more** energy. It is associated with movement and strength.

As the body operates, there is a shift of energy as any reaction within is followed by a measurable and important loss of energy. A decrease of energy in our body affects the body, the mind and the soul negatively because the energy required for a healthy and strong organism is thus reduced. The body, soul and mental creativity weaken and decrease in productivity if the lost energy is not made up quickly. To make up for this spent energy, new energy must constantly be supplied to the body and soul if constant physical health and greater productivity of the mind is to be sustained.

When energy diminishes or is lacking in the physical body, the body's organs and systems stop working properly which cause internal disharmony. In extreme circumstances, a specific organ may stop functioning. A decrease in performance of one functioning organ could potentially lead to the demise of organs that greatly depend on the specific role and/or finished product (hormone) of the demised organ to continue performing efficiently. We must remember that all organs depend on each other to keep us healthy. Therefore, this chain of organ weakness or failure may continue from one low performing organ to the next as long as the problem remains. Ultimately, the whole body system gets jammed, leading ultimately to illness because the organs that connect the various body systems are no longer functioning in harmony. A total lack of energy in the body for some time will surely result in the death of some amount of body cells. The person may end up losing his or her life unless immediate care is provided. In sum, energy is so important in our life cycle that we must keep a close watch to it.

The sources of energy

There are four ways a person acquires energy.

1. We have the **parental energy** that is given to us at birth by our parents. This type is determined by how healthy our parents were during the time of conception and also our mother's health state during pregnancy, taking in consideration any

complications or birth defects including the physical environment surrounding the pregnancy.

2. In addition, there is the **acquired energy,** energy obtained the inherited way, the essential you. This is largely determined by the general constitution of one's family and depends if, in our family tree, there are certain conditions existing such as Alzheimer, diabetes, heart disease etc., though they may skip a generation.

3. There is the **energy derived through spiritual means**, by way of prayers, spells, incantations, meditations, intense thought directed to oneself, concentration, inspirational readings, music, etc. This energy most likely strengthens the soul while solidifying the mind; the soul in return strengthens the body.

4. Finally, we have the **acquired energy**, which derives from our diets, our physical endurance and environmental conditions (e.g., food, fluids, air and

exercise). In general, knowing about what kind of acquired energy we possess is primordial to understanding our own health.

Now that we have an understanding of the importance of energy for our overall health, it would be wise to also be equally aware of how our energy can be drained, exposing us to health issues.

What depletes the energy within the body?

Energy is the life force within our body. It is the driving force that propels us to wake up every morning and go about our business with vitality and endurance. Without this energy, our body gets weaker and our strength diminishes. It should then be to our advantage to learn what depletes that energy in our life so that we can exert control over it.

Certainly, little or no food for some time will deplete our body's energy. Too little or too much sexual intercourse can deplete the energy in the body. Unhealthy food and beverages, unsafe drinking water and other fluids would also drain our energy. Lack of exercise or too much exercise, the excessive use or abuse of drugs and alcohol can also reduce energy in our body as can too much or too little sexual intercourse. Exposure to too much heat, too much cold, and too much wind, all of which are physical stressors, will also decrease our body's supply of energy. Emotional or mental stress, anxiety, spiritual warfare, be it chronic or temporary, all deplete our body's energy as well and increasing the likelihood that we will become sick.

Fortunately, diet is the most crucial element in providing energy for the body for we can exert maximum control over what we ingest. A good diet leads to a healthy person while a poor diet leads to all kinds of sicknesses and diseases. A healthy diet provides nutrients that help your body produce the energy needed for a healthy life cycle whereas a poor diet will produce little or no energy, reducing your body's flow of energy, weakening it and rendering it vulnerable to disease. Without question, dietary imbalances are the leading preventable contributors to premature death around the world.

And, with living and working conditions being what they are in our twenty-first century, stress is a major contributing factor to most of our bodily energy imbalances.

Stress and its importance.

Stress is the adaptive response of the body, mind and soul to demands and needs made on them. Any needs in our life, any short or long term plans, responsibilities or duties give us stress. Providing and protecting our family produces stresses on our physical, mental and spiritual bodies. Any change in our life (e.g., job loss, job search, marriage, divorce, new born baby, new boss, spiritual awakening,) stresses us intensely. The stress is expressly visible in our physical body as it bears the demand to act on the challenges it faces. It would also be seen in our spirit by people blessed with third eye vision. We cannot avoid stress; it is part of our life. Without stress, life would be without excitement and color. As the driving force of our life, we all need a certain amount of stress to impel creativity, innovation, change and inspiration. Stress could be considered a necessary force for mankind's achievements.

On the other hand, stress can have a negative effect on human health when uncontrolled. It can be extremely damaging to our health when accumulated, or when several stressful events occur simultaneously or within a relatively short period of time. Too much stress will deplete our energy, making us sick.

It is worth mentioning that during times of stress, the heart rate might increase. Since the primary role of the heart is to pump the blood at a certain rate of speed the volume of blood pumped could eventually increase as well. This situation can lead to high blood pressure. And the heart rate may more than double the normal heart beat.

It should be noted that high blood pressure can damage tissues of the heart, brain, kidneys and other organs which could lead to insomnia, restless nights, strokes, kidney failure, and heart disease. Stress also attacks the immune system. Digestive problems often develop when our resistance is low.

Because stress is a necessary evil, stepping back from our daily stresses in life may bring peace of mind and restore the flow of energy in our bodies. Therefore, we must learn how to deal with stress, balancing the need to be healthy yet productive at the same time.

Holistic treatment versus allopathic treatment.

While the "allopathic view" of treatment targets the disease and its symptoms, the "holistic view" targets the cause of the malady. As an example, if you suffer a headache, the allopathic treatment will prescribe medicine only for your headache whereas the holistic treatment will be focus on the reason you have a headache in the first place. Allopathic treatment only focuses on the malady and its obvious symptoms without considering any mental or emotional dimension that may be involved. The holistic view considers your body, your mind, your soul, your diet and your life style.

The definition of soul loss

The soul may detach from the body and wander while we are dreaming or sleeping and even if awake. This phenomenon is known in the spiritual world as an "out of body experience" and is considered normal when the soul returns to the physical body. But problems only occur when for some reason, the soul cannot find its way back into the body or chooses not to return to it; if this happens, there is soul loss.

Soul loss may also be caused by a ghost attempting to draw the soul away from a person for its own reasons. It may be due to witchcraft or evil spirits attempting to take dominion over the person's body for manipulative purposes. Most soul loss cases occur when one sustains a painful physical injury to the body or experiences a life threatening event and the person's soul leaves the body as a result.

When the soul permanently leaves the body, it usually heads to the land of the dead; the closer it gets, the weaker the body it left becomes. Eventually, if nothing is done for the return of the soul, the person dies.

The meaning of spirit attachment

Spirit attachment occurs when a spirit attaches itself to a living human being much like a parasite, and possesses it. Symptoms of spirit attachment include depression, mood swings, multiple personality disorders and sudden changes of behavior, sometimes radical. The spirit mostly attaches itself to the person's aura.

The origins of sickness and their symptoms

The definitions of soul loss and spirit attachment above were given to assist the reader through the spiritual nature of the next chapters.

The intent of this writing is to shed light on the role of the soul, which is hugely underestimated in our well being.

The soul interacts with the spiritual world. Although unseen by average people who cannot see their soul with their naked eyes, the soul is there with us, in us, always. Like our physical body, our soul has needs, demands, desires and wishes.

According to ancient beliefs, some of our stress may originate from our soul's needs or demands. If the soul's needs are not being addressed properly or at all, the soul can enter into depression or stress out and the worries from the soul can cause sudden stress on the physical body without warning. In fact, the soul lives and has times of happiness, unhappiness, times for action, periods of awareness, and times that it has issues that need to be addressed. The physical body is the channel the soul uses through which to express itself.

When it becomes clear that some sicknesses, either diagnosed or unknown, are incurable after several vigorous treatments, the traditional healer's belief is that it is only then wise to use all possible alternative medicines available in combinations. Having understood that the soul is a unique separate entity to be dealt with, in accordance with its unique spiritual laws, the spiritual gurus humbly advise adding an alternative way of getting better by treating ourselves wholely, due to the complex inter-relationship between the body, the mind and the soul.

They believe that the cause of the illness may be linked to the patient's soul or mind and emotions, which exert influence over the body so that proper care would address them as well as the physical for overall health.

The relationship between the soul and the body including their shared symptoms

It is said that we have diseases that affect the body as well as diseases that affect the soul and we also have diseases that affect the mind. The question is, how can we separate the mind from the soul or the body and vice versa?

Diseases that affect the soul are attached on the soul. They have dominion on the spiritual level but, until we have a scientific breakthrough that can detect them, they can only be seen through spiritual eyes.

According to African and other common traditional beliefs, the basic ways to cure any spiritual ill and heal the soul is to undergo spiritual cleansings, meditation, fasting, prayers and intercession including physical detoxification.

When the disease is truly residing in the soul, the reaction or symptoms would be visible and noticeable through the physical body. Often, the symptoms presented are mistaken as arising out of physical disease and are treated as such due to their similarities to such; but in fact, the illness originated in the soul but the physical body is the only tool the soul has to draw attention to any spiritual impairment needing care. Whatever evil or ill in the soul would also then be felt in the body as well to signal that something is wrong and that action is required.

Note that any bad feeling or pain might seem like a physical one (or exactly the same as how it felt when your body hurt due to a physical cause) but in reality, the illness lies in your soul. Hence, no one can be blamed for not correctly identifying the source, as it is extremely difficult to be able to tell where the pain originates unless you are closely keeping up with your dreams and visions and can intercept some signal from the spirit.

Since the soul lives in the body and is connected to it, they share the same pains and feelings. For a patient presenting physical symptoms originating from a spiritually-related illness, modern prescriptions may not be completely effective as the disease resides in the soul. The symptoms may disappear for a short time due to the intake of medicine but they will reappear at some point since the disease remains truly untreated in the soul.

The connection to understand here is the relation between the soul and the body. If one of them is hurting or suffering, it undoubtedly affects the other. The body and the soul have the same identical shape and form and anything affecting the one affects the other simultaneously.

It might be necessary to explain why I say the soul is identical to the physical body in shape and traits. If you have ever dreamed during your sleep, it is that other you that looks like you and fully representing you in that spiritual world of your sleep that I call the soul. Some dreams might feel so real that we only take notice it was actually a dream when we wake up. Our "double" that acts on our behalf in the spiritual world looks identical to the person in the physical world. If you take a close look at your soul during your dreams, you will agree that the soul does looks like you in your dreams with all your body parts. Can't we therefore conclude that the soul has body parts just like us?

According to spiritual understandings, most spiritual attacks or spells are always directed to the spiritual body. Depending on the anatomical parts in your soul that are affected during a spiritual attack, it will subsequently lead to the same pain in your physical body in those exact locations as in your soul. If your soul's legs are hurting, it will result to your body feeling the same pain physically in the legs also.

So consider that if you have been unwell or not feeling very good or having allergies for some unknown reasons, and have tried to cure or ease them, it could well be that what's wrong is actually residing in your soul rather than your body, which would explain why, after so much time, some sickness or pain is chronic and may seem like a death sentence as we always find ourselves the victim of the same diseases and pains over and over again, despite a false, all too short recovery.

The relationship between the body and the soul.

According to ancient beliefs and understandings, when your body is in pain, it also affects your soul, causing your soul to feel the same pain as your body.

As long as your pain continues, your soul will also be in pain, jointly with your body. It is exactly the same scenario described in the chapters above. The difference is that the origin of the disease is in this case the body.

One important aspect to remember is our discussion concerning your soul's ability to leave or depart from your body both while sleeping and in some cases while awake, in order to free itself from the shared uneasy connection to the body during physical sickness. That might be the soul's mechanism of coping, as it seeks help or as it takes a step back to figure out how it can assist the body.

In some extreme circumstances, where the pain is unbearable, the soul may depart from the body until the illness is taken care of or the pain eases. The soul will be on standby, hanging around for some time out of the body, the only way it knows not to feel or share the body's pain. The shorter the pain or illness, the shorter the time the soul will either wander or stick it out and remain residing in the body. If our health worsens, our soul may begin to wander and wander further away from the body. It may end up traveling deep into vast spiritual realms and could potentially become a lost soul.

Realizing that our body cannot live long on earth or stay mentally stable without a soul, it follows that our body or body part could cease to function, or, we may go insane and in the worse case scenario we might enter into a coma or lose our precious life. This situation could create a condition resulting in gradual death of the body or the body part if there is a disconnection of a partial withdrawal of the soul from the body, in which case, the soul might be nearby, barely hanging onto the unbalanced physical body.

As the soul wanders, either in an attempt to return to its body or as it seeks a solution, it will encounter obstacles in the other worlds. The spiritual realm is full of mysterious wonders that are fully alive and essential. There are a lot of spiritual worlds and each one of them is a separate entity where the soul can easily forget how to find its way back to the body without a spiritual guide.

Every individual's case and each experience is differently perceived and differently lived according to one's mental level and level of spirituality on awakening.

People who are spiritually rooted and mentally strong may have a different outcome, primarily because they will most likely be aware of their dreams and visions and probably be already taking action to assist their soul by opting alternative means to get well with an open mind.

The realm of the living and the non-living

Following the same scenario as stated in the previous chapter, if the soul, unable to endure a lengthy sickness or extreme physical pain, leaves the body, it could, in some cases, wander out of reach if it has traveled too deeply into the spiritual world. In some instances the wandering soul can lose its way in the spiritual world or find itself stranded by other spiritual living beings. Its endurance could fade away in that spiritual world with the potential result that the soul strays farther away from the person's physical or mental reach. Ultimately, the soul, in hopeless despair, might stop trying to return to the body or it may lack the ability to return. The result is the slow death of the body or the development of mental disorders.

I grew up in Burkina Faso, West Africa, where there is a popular belief that people who are mentally unstable may have been the victim of a soul loss. It was common to hear it said of them, "His/her soul was out of the body" or "His/her soul is outside." I'm sure there could be other explanations as well.

Let's suppose that a friend who was sick recuperates and returns to physical health so that his/her soul returns from the spiritual world even after a period of wandering or after having been standing watch nearby. In this case, the soul will once again rest happily in a healthy body without needing any further care.

But, in this same scenario, imagine the soul not able to return to the body because it has already crossed the bridge between life and death or, according to African and Indian tribal belief, because it is being held in the spiritual world against its will. This situation will leave your friend's body healthy again, but on earth without a soul. In the latter case, your friend's body will eventually die; whether death comes sooner or later will depend on the state of your friend's mental strength and spiritual affiliations for, ultimately, no body can survive without a soul under peril of becoming mentally instable or, perhaps worse yet, surviving but possessed by another spirit.

The wandering soul, traveling from place to place during the time of sickness, either overcoming obstacles or fighting to survive, may get jailed, kidnapped, stranded in a strange land, beaten, frightened or literally subdued to the point that it becomes exhausted. This is usually in the case when a ghost attempts to draw the soul away. The good news is that these events may appear to us in our dreams, visions or nightmares and our body (mind) will feel/know them because of their familiar connection to our soul. We might dream and wake up sweaty, frightened, scared with a jump, hitting the wall, even breaking fingers or arms or just seeing ourself in a dream being chased after and literally fighting for our life as our soul is truly sensing danger. It could become a struggle for survival through challenges the soul is facing in the spiritual realm. These spiritual insights are signs that our soul is struggling to survive and to keep up with it's consign body. The soul in connection with the mind is attempting to warn the body (mind) via dreams and visions that its life is threatened and we must act promptly to find a solution. In some cases, friends or family members may have dreams or visions concerning the person who needs urgent help.

If we are spiritually and mentally strong, our soul may fight its way to the body to rest though it may be tired, exhausted, beaten up or even injured; the battle may still not be over even though our soul has returned to its consigned body. Our soul may still need spiritual healings and spiritual feedings to replenish the lost energy. You may think that since the soul literally cannot die, it is immune to feelings and emotions, but in reality, to be healthy, the soul needs as much care and nurturing as our physical body.

While in the strange spiritual world, fighting and encountering other spiritual living beings and the souls of dead people, the soul may sometimes (though seldom) make its way back to the body with some new and foreign spiritual living beings attached to it or with negative energy that it deposits into the physical body. In such cases, the physical body or mind that had healed will react to these new and foreign living beings now attached or residing into the soul and a new illness may start.

Our body would now experience the same feelings and emotions in the same way that our consign soul is experiencing them as, again, our body is connected to our soul and our soul is connected to our body. Feelings of anxiety, stress, sadness, pain, sickness, and paranoia may directly be linked to our soul's feelings and emotions. According to some African spirituals beliefs, any attempt to cure these maladies through modern technology would most likely be ineffective as the real evil and its symptoms originate in our soul, not our physical body.

In summary, while taking care of our body during sickness, we should simultaneously take care of our soul to better fight against evil and diseases existing in the universe that affect all our aspects: our spirit, mind and body. Conversely, while focusing on our soul's health, the mind cannot be excluded as it simultaneously grows in character and strength.

Laws of the universe applied to human bodily functions.

The physical or natural world is governed by invisible forces or laws that follow and complement one another, cycle after cycle in perfect harmony. Our universe is made of innumerable materials, yet they all work together in a natural structure of perfect cause and effect. It is as if the universe is a giant machine that faithfully adheres to auto control that it has set itself on. Through the laws imposed on it, there is balanced maintained.

For example, the mechanical structure in place for rain to fall on earth never fails to deliver as long as all the requirements for natural rain are met. The sun heats the ocean and lakes which causes the water to evaporate. The heated water invisibly mixes with the air that gradually rises higher as the sun continues to heat the water creating increased evaporation. This phenomenon forms clouds filled with water that falls down when the clouds condense and become dense enough to cause rainfall. The same cycle has repeated itself forever and still follows the same exact natural procedure while producing the same effect.

This natural structure is applied to all natural phenomena, and all follow the laws of nature. Phenomena such as wind, hurricane, storms, drought, earthquakes and tsunamis will occur inevitably as soon as all the conditions required by the laws of nature are met. There is no holding back and no chance of non-compliance with the laws of nature. This is what I mean when I say that everything in the universe works in perfect order respecting the law of cause and effect law that governs the natural world. Since the beginning of time, this law, which has variously been called the law of attraction, gravity, or supernatural forces, never fails to deliver the expected and preordained effect.

Ultimately, every particle of matter needs the others if it is to perform a complete cycle. When changes or obstacles present themselves, changes will occur in the results. These natural forces are unconcerned as to whether their effects on living beings in the universe are good or bad, positive or negative. The natural phenomena lack feeling and emotions, for their role and their importance is only to produce the expected effects that arise from the given causes; collateral damages that are a by-product of their effect does not concerned them. It follows that if all the conditions for a hurricane are met, then the hurricane will happened without concern about the houses or cars or living beings displaced. Any destructive consequence that follows after the hurricane will only be sad news for whoever is its victim.

Living beings in the universe seem to be powerless to control how they are affected by these natural phenomena. Humans are left with no other choice but to learn to adapt and live a healthy life despite these natural phenomena occurring.

Though we cannot change the universal natural laws initially put in place, we can manipulate the law of cause and effect by understanding which factors cause various events to occur and in what circumstances. Only then can we work our way to inducing a voluntary cause to produce the effect we desire that will benefit us positively while being mindful of our environment. By understanding how natural phenomena work, we can attempt to take - and should take - positive steps to both heal and also better protect nature and our universe by inducing positive causes.

Through this understanding, we can technically find a way of exerting some control over weather and other natural phenomena to a certain extent and to better predict their occurrence before they take place.

The main point of the above discussion of the infallible laws governing the universe is to focus us on the physiology of the human body that forms a single block of body, with various organs and different complex systems that work together, connected as a whole in perfect harmony to allow a state of health just as the universe, in its complex composition, never fails the law of cause and effect.

So, if all the conditions are present in an individual to experience a stroke, then that individual will have a stroke without fail and this is true until the cause and effect for a stroke renders a different outcome. The same goes with all and any diseases; once all their prerequisites and conditions are present within any human body (cause), the person powerlessly starts showing symptoms equivalent to the exact effect. The question about how good or bad for the body (the person) is not asked in this situation since the disease will not wait for your consent before showing symptoms. We call it a disease but in truth it could be presented as a phenomenon that has taken place within your body. A phenomenon that has arisen based on the cause and effect laws just like in the universe presented above. It is without question that there exists within the body a system of law and order that maintains all the organs and their systems together in harmony to keep the body whole and healthy. If there is a breach in any of the systems and their connections, the body is going to react to the breach and try to restore order within it and at the same time, the effect that the breach has caused will be shown or displayed as symptoms as there exist some irregularities in the order that guarantees health. The question one would ask will be, what has caused the disharmony? Once you find the cause, it becomes easier to take precautions for the breach not to happen again if staying healthy is the goal. The sole solution is to understand the causes for the illness and reverse them to induce a healthy result while maintaining a healthy life style.

The human body is made of a connection of atoms to molecules, to cells and tissues then to organs that are connected to one another through a chain of systems. Each organ has a specific role in our well-being. If an organ is disconnected from the system, the entire chain connecting all the other body organs will be affected negatively by that lack of connection.

For perfect or total health to exist, all our bodily organs have to work properly and work together in harmony. Usually, illness occurs when there is disharmony between the organs and their related cells or function. Illness is often due to blockages or obstacles in the flow of energy within. In that case the organ may stop functioning properly causing the person to become ill or experience fatigue. It follows then, that in considering the health of the digestive system, we should take into account all the organs that ensure it works properly and confirm they are in perfect health and exist in harmony.

To summarize, health is the combination of proper functioning of the organs within their specific system to ensure a good flow of fluids, nutrients and energy throughout the whole body. If we are to cure illness, we must always target the illness from the source rather than only treating the symptoms. Only by targeting the main cause, will we influence the effect positively by curing the illness and reestablishing a good flow in the connection between organs.

Is this headache caused from the stomach, spleen or kidneys? It is possible that it is caused by an organ in the circulatory system or the digestive system. Likewise, eye problems may find their origin in a liver that is not functioning well and swollen feet in the kidney that needs attention. The objective in treating the body as a whole is to put back harmony and increase the flow of energy, rejuvenating the body through activation of the body's natural healing powers.

Just as in the universe all things have a function, so everything in our body has been created to perform a specific duty and follows natural laws that all the organs and their systems must follow in order to keep the body healthy. We know that our emotions and thoughts may adversely affect our health; likewise, any other threat to the body's optimal functioning must also come from external contact.

If we then consider our physical body separate from our mental and spiritual bodies, we would conclude that our body is nothing more than a machine that needs food, water and energy to keep running and maintain our body's cellular function working. Perhaps this explains why some people may have a good working physical body yet may lack a healthy mental or spiritual body.

However, viewing our physical body as a living, talking, machine, it becomes clear that without our mental and spiritual bodies, our physical body may be without movements and creativity. Life would not be balanced or even possible; we would simply have a live body, but a body without life.

With this understanding, we can conclude that we are not the physical body, but rather, we are the mental and spiritual bodies because without those bodies, the physical body alone has no life. The physical body is the host body while the mental and spiritual bodies are actually life. It is for this reason that in addition to eating healthy food and providing healthy nutrients to keep the physical body healthy, our health is affected, adversely or positively, by our emotions, thoughts and our spiritual dimensions.

Unspoken laws determining our future physical health

Everything in the universe is mathematically calculable. Our moves, our actions, our walking, even talking can be summed up in numbers. The fact that the world, in all its aspects, can be reduced to numbers is a determining fact: everything in the universe is relative. Everything is always conditioned on a precedent action that is mathematically calculable according to how, when, why, how many, how strong, how weak, how deep, how long... the precedent action has impact. Everything is relative to the forces behind any action or any effect. Whether the forces are strong, mild, or weak will show in the result, based on its relativity. Everything obeys the laws according to its weight, length, depth, size, distance, strength, width, position, etc.

The whole universe is built in a mathematical consciousness so nothing is out of proportion and the universe as a whole remains in balance and perfect harmony. Nothing comes from nothing, and all things have to always come from something as a result of some initial thing. This immutable universe is the result of so many primary causes that are taking effect according and always in relation to the first cause. Every single cause produces its unique effect proportionally and the same causes produce inevitably the same effects.

As part of this universe, we humans are subject to the same law. Everything in our individual life is also relative to prior causes. That includes our health.

Everything in our physical body can be mathematically calculated and reduced to numbers. Human life involves a mathematical form that can be calculated at any given time. The right numbers describe good health; any number that deviates from the right numbers causes an adverse effect in your health. You need a certain amount of food, fluids, nutrients and vitamins relative to your weight and height, both of which can be mathematically calculated. Every organ needs a certain amount of oxygen, energy, blood and water that is just right to properly function. The system of organs that form the organism as a whole has to flow within and connect to one another without any disruption in between.

The exact amount of each is needed for healthy function of your physical body.

If all body organs and their systems in the chain of connections are exactly the way a normal physical body should be, then you have perfect and complete health proportionate to the related numbers. If there is any irregularity in the required amounts - no matter how small and whether high or low - everything else along the chain will change accordingly as a result in the effect. We would have a relative condition of health that conforms to the changes in numbers.

In applying mathematics to health, we can detect and prevent any foreseeable potential disharmony within the body system by comparing the normal numbers (volume, quantity, size, etc.) to see if the numbers remain stable, rise or decline. The number cannot be lower or higher than that for normal health or illness will occur relative to what corresponding degree the organs would be affected.

Following the same logical conclusion, namely that numbers govern human health, all things within our body are inter-related and interconnected and all things act or react proportionate to the initial cause. This means that our weight, height, including our body organs strength and health, blood flow, airflow, even the slightest itch we feel are all related to a primary cause.

The universe as a whole governs itself automatically through numbers, cycle after cycle and so does our human body. If we eat, drink, and breathe healthfully in combination with the right exercise, it will cause good body health; and if we don't, that too will show its effect. In health, everything is relative and our health respects the law of relativity just as the universe does.

Importantly, the energy required within our body can also be calculated in numbers. A certain amount of energy is required for a healthy flow within our body organ systems. The right number in our energy level is needed to cause a perfect health. This number is based on our weight, height and our organs' strength and is important to know so that our whole body can align itself with the right number. When the number in our energy level is either higher or lower, the health of our body is affected relatively, according to the excess or lack of energy. Based on our body weight and height, we are supposed to have in circulation a certain amount of energy for a healthy flow; if there is a deviation, an imbalance will result and the body's health would be relatively affected accordingly. When there is more energy than is needed, there are health consequences as well, which are proportionate to how high that number is.

It is crucial to realize and remember that energy is the most important element for our long-term prognosis of health. If we don't control the amount of energy we burn on a daily basis in our younger ages and replenish it in the right amounts, we cause our body to weaken as we grow old, eventually lowering our immune system's ability to fight off disease.

In summary, our human physical body is mathematically built based on numbers and everything that exists within our body system works as part of a whole and is relatively connected.

The invisible wire and its relationship to the body.

It is known that within our body there is another body of sorts. Imagine a wire or an invisible circuit within us, most commonly called the energy field. It has our body form and is responsible for the health of our body, which depends on its position within us. If that wire, which is living, is not resting in its system comfortably to ensure a fine flow of energy within, the body organs and their system of connections will not be in harmony. For perfect health, this wire that surrounds our body's ins and outs has to conform exactly to the shape of our physical body shape. This wire is what keeps our entire body and all it's organs in good condition and balanced within in energy flow.

If, for some reason, our wire or invisible circuit happens to move, either upward or downward or shifts from its comfortable, conforming position, our physical body weakens and we eventually becomes sick or depressed.

To better understand the mechanism of the wire, it is necessary to check our body's standard posture to assess how strong our muscles and ligaments are joined together in keeping our skeleton body and joints as a whole solid so as to ensure a proper alignment of the said wire. The stronger and better-positioned that wire inside our body is, the stronger and healthier we are.

We now have scientific proof that our human body is surrounded by an electromagnetic field called an "aura," which protects our body from harmful negative energy in the universe. It is also proven that when spanning from the infrared to the ultraviolet light of a sick person's aura, the lower frequency portion of the spectrum seems to be related to the low level of functioning parts of the body that needed care.

At this point we have proof that there is more to discover concerning our human physical body.

Our energy field (wire), connected to our aura is part of our body's energy anatomy.

The wire facilitates the flow of energy within our body. We should then understand that there must exist a specific and clear-cut route within us to allow the energy to be channeled to all parts of the body. The energy must flow smoothly in order to nourish our body effectively. When there are blockages within the channel of energy (along the route), the flow, speed, volume, and timing of delivering energy to all parts of our body are affected leaving our body and its organs unsatisfied. In that case, our body is not being getting the energy as it requires and as expected for healthy functioning of all the organs and their systems. If the blockage is not removed or adjusted, our body would have to cope and we might eventually get sick or experience discomfort as long as the blockage remains.

As our body organs are connected to one another, when an organ fails to perform due to insufficient energy, the next organ that depends on that organ's effectiveness to do it's task will suffer and provide low services thereby worsening our health.

The relationship between the energy field, the mind and the body.

Let us consider the holistic view that sickness occurs internally as a result of disharmony between our organs and the emotions we have that are often related to imbalances within the organs' energy. This section will focus on the imbalances in our organs' energy as relates to our inner invisible body or second body, our energy field, through our mind. When our inner invisible body is affected, it affects the health of our physical body. The inner invisible body reduces its energy flow or, in some circumstances, becomes affected by associated emotions. As we said, when the inner invisible body moves or changes its normal natural position by shifting upwards, downwards, or reposition itself within for adaptation mainly due to external or internal pressure, the physical internal body structures and organization in energy distribution are correspondingly affected. Emotions associated with an organ are the fundamental idea of Chinese medicine. For example grief is the emotion of the lungs and the large intestine that will often trigger a cold and a feeling of energetically being drained, sometimes accompanied with difficulty to have a bowel movement. Happiness and joy are the emotions of the heart and the small intestine and when we express these emotions, we are nourishing our heart and small intestinal energy and we can see our life experiences clearly with a clear mind.

Our invisible inner body is responsible for the health and well being of our physical, internal energy. The greater that energy flow pulls, or moves in a way that is adverse to a positive energy flow, the greater the damage to the stored energy of organs in our physical body as it will have to adapt within its own circuit. Even then, it will deliver insufficient energy or will not deliver the energy in a timely fashion, thereby causing our body organs to adapt to these changes, all of which are not in the best interest of our health. In doing so, the physical body is following the laws relating to the cause-effect connection between mind, body and soul. Our inner invisible body is affected by our thoughts, our remorse and joys and our environment and reflects its state in the mind and in the soul. It is like the direct link to the outside world; how we treat ourselves and others, how we think and how our surroundings affect our mind and soul stabilities. It is true that positive thinking and good deeds encourage good health as these contribute to good energy flow thereby having a beneficial impact on our inner body. Negative thinking and bad deeds, on the other hand, cause blockage within our energy flow affecting our inner body negatively. This could be due to feelings of remorse associated with these negative modes or connected to the laws of karma. Thus, if we want the energy flow in our inner body to be physically healthy, we must keep our thoughts, deeds and emotions positive.

The symptoms of the different sicknesses linked to internal thoughts and emotions are often similar to those experienced in the physical body from causes that are external. In both cases, there is an imbalance in our body's organs. In both cases, these symptoms are linked to the inability of our inner invisible body to effectively perpetuate its energy and channel it throughout our physical body organs.

To summarize, any disharmony in our inner invisible body or energy field will make its way to the organs of the physical body because of their connection. Due to the similarity of symptoms, it could become difficult to diagnose the origin of the symptoms and how to alleviate them.

Examples of life phenomena that display the same symptoms as physically-originated maladies even though their origin lies elsewhere: spiritual attacks, blockages in the aura field, spirit attachment, a ghost attempting to draw someone's soul out of the physical body, a soul out of the body due to near death experiences and stress.

If we are serious about maintaining good health, it is wise to keep in mind these ideas when treating one who is sick, remembering that the patient's presented symptoms may have originated in an organ other than the organ displaying symptoms or they may be directly linked to the patient's mental and emotional state or to external spiritual attacks creating imbalances in the energy flow.

At the end of the day, when you realize what you need to be a healthy human being and why, consider everything else that makes the universe as a whole run well. As without certain good conditions prevalent the universe itself will show effects, so too, our health in general will be in jeopardy when conditions are unfavorable.

On the bright side, sickness can give birth to spiritual awakening and afford us the desire to understand and discover who we are and, most importantly, raise our eyes to the Creator as we seek answers and divine help in our despair, prepared to turn our full attention to what we can learn for our health, knowledge and understanding.

The aura

The aura is the electromagnetic field of energy that surrounds our human body as well as that of any living entity (animal, plants, and trees) and even inanimate objects such as a chair. The aura is a unique energy system that protects us from harmful (negative) energy in the universe. The size of an aura may vary from a few inches to spanning many feet or miles in all directions. The aura, like our fingerprints, is unique to each individual. It is like a multicolored mist comprising seven layers of vital energy that radiate through the human body and each layer has its specific function distinguishing it from the other layers. Each layer is a different color, which will vary and change depending upon our mental, emotional and physical state. The colors also indicate the strength of our immune system and our authentic self, exposing our hidden character to those able to see auras. It is known that the seventh layer of the aura of spiritual leaders is often bright and there is sometime a circle over their head in a golden color similar to a halo.

The importance of the aura in connection to the body.

The aura protects our body and its cells from negative energy from the universe surrounding us for, some energy in the universe may be harmful to our health when exposed to it. Keep in mind that energy is also discharged and received on our earth from other planets and galaxies above and beyond. The aura is like our spiritual super man shield, blocking any negative energy from harming our body. The aura is the extension from the energy field within the body to the outside spiritual world wrapped up around the physical body from head to toe like a nut within its shell. It protects us from negative energy, from spells and from spiritual attacks directed from our fellow man as well as from animals, plants and any other source. The aura, as a shield, and an envelope, surrounding our bodies is first in contact with the external world and if there is any dirt in our way, it will fall on the aura first. That's why it is imperative to dust ourselves off from those energies from time to time in order to make room for the new one energy.

Our aura also supplies our body with positive energy as it prevents harmful negative energy from penetrating the body. It is the protective shield that keeps us healthy and joyful by repelling negative energy. Our personal aura, in its size and magnitude is associated with our physical health and the health of all our organs. As our aura represents and exposes the health status of our physical body to the world, it is said that spiritual gurus can see it with their spiritual eyes and interpret it based on its brightness.

However, stress and illness will adversely affect the aura. Certain diseases can cause gaps in our aura. When something blocks the energy flow within the aura, our protective shield weakens, making us unhappy, depressed, or sick. It is known that to restore the aura, cleansing it may be effective. One way to do this is with exercise techniques such as stretching, bending and flexing.

Relationship between the aura, the mind and the body to the universe.

The status of our physical health affects our aura. Anything that affects our human body negatively will also affect our aura negatively. Any negative energy from the physical external world affects the aura.

In addition, our moods, emotions, feelings, thoughts and intentions affect the aura.

There is irony here, for while the health of our physical body depends to a great extent on our moods, emotions, thoughts, intentions and internal energy flow, our moods, our emotions, our thoughts, and our energy flow may be adversely affected by our physical health when exposed to external evils of the world. This is solid proof that the processes of thought and emotion, and our bodies are interrelated and dynamic.

It followed then that total and perfect health must involve our physical health, our mental health and our spiritual health. And that total and perfect health centers on the sum of our feelings, our emotions, our thoughts and our life style including our spiritual dimension.

In summation, we must agree that illness results from either external causes or internal disharmony between the organs and their associated emotions, most often related to imbalances in the energy of our organs.

The aura, in protecting us from unwanted energy that exists in the universe gives rise to the knowledge that our universe is filled with energy. As human beings in this universe, with any movement, if we are walking, standing, running or anything else, we are subject to the law of gravity. While gravity is pulling us down, normal force is pushing us up and air pressure is pressing at us from all sides. And you should note that normal force is actually geometry. It's the force that supports the weight of an object on a surface and we should be grateful for this force because it is that force that keeps you from falling through the floor. Thanks to the combination of these forces, we are able to walk and stand up without falling, and run while still keeping our balance. We are able to enjoy these actions made possible because of a certain natural structure set up during creation.

The importance of cleansing the aura and its related symptoms.

We are always in contact with other people's auras in our daily life without realizing it or paying attention to it. Our body aura mingles and enters into contact with the auras of our co-workers, family members, friends and pedestrians' while we interact with the world. Every time an aura contacts another aura, they both will wash out one another and connect by exchanging energies. During our regular daily course of life, we collect energy from the other people we contact. These different energies may be negative and when they are, they will, in the long run, have a negative effect on our general well being. We are also exposed to different and potentially harmful energies coming from natural life such as the earth itself, the sun, oceans, mountains, plants and the animals of the universe.

As we are mindful of our personal hygiene, taking a daily bath to wash away dirt and the sweat accumulated, so too, as we accumulate unwanted energies in daily life that are deposited on our aura, regular cleansing of our aura will support our well-being. As a person with poor hygienic may become sick or unpleasant to others, if we do not clean our aura, it will become dirtier and dirtier until we become sick or unpleasant to others. From a spiritual point of view, that is what happens when we don't like someone on first sight for no apparent reason, or when do not feel comfortable in a given place and have the desire to leave as soon as possible, simply to evacuate the area. When our aura is cleansed, it guarantees a smooth flow of positive energy throughout the whole body keeping us healthy and happy. Most importantly a healthy aura attracts positive energy making us likable to everyone.

There are various symptoms that would show us that it is time to have a spiritual bath.

Symptoms that prove you may have attachments on your aura and need cleansing.

- You are easily irritated, agitated and feel rage;
- You have low energy, lack energy and feel lazy;
- You are easily distracted and cannot focus on one thing in a given time;
- You constantly worry and live in fear;
- You have a lot of inner voices and inner conflicts;
- You have little or no motivation for life;
- You have suicidal thoughts.

From the point of view of a healer, all disease originates from blockages in the energetic anatomy. When the energetic blockage is cleared via the auric cleansing, the physical disease disappears. It is said that meditation is the best way to improve the aura.

According to ancient belief and spiritual knowledge, we have the Chakras and the Meridians along with the aura. These constitute some major other parts of our spiritual energy anatomy.

In brief, chakras and meridians are as important as the aura. They contribute to our overall health and our strength of mind and spirit in connection with the universe and the Creator. They are also link and attached to our body organs and other key parts of the body and play a huge role in balancing our mind, body and soul energetically and harmoniously. The human spiritual anatomy is a great field to explore, as it will uncover an abundance of secret advantages to your health.

Imperative rules of wellness

Since we cannot change the laws of nature, we must live and abide by them.

Life is itself governed by laws. To live a good, healthy life requires knowledge of those laws and living by them with understanding. Life is freely given to us but to keep it and to live well, we must live according to the different laws that apply to us with faithfulness and understanding, or sickness, anxiety, stress, restless nights, a lack of inner peace and a premature death will be our inevitable sentence.

At every point in our life we should be mindful and there are things we should always consider.

He who does not control what goes into his mouth is not ready to be healthy;

He who does not care about what goes into his mouth is not ready to be healthy;

He who does not select what goes into his mouth is not ready to be healthy;

He who is not aware of what goes into his mouth is not ready to be healthy.

He who does not know what is good and healthy for his body is not ready to be healthy:

He who does not control what comes out of his mouth is not ready for spiritual growth;

He who does not care what comes out of his mouth is not ready for a spiritual growth;

He who does not select what comes out of his mouth is not ready for spiritual growth;

He who is not aware of what comes out of his mouth is not ready for spiritual growth;

He who does not know what is good and healthy for his body, soul and mind is not ready for spiritual growth;

Spiritual growth means taking your life under control, taking your mind under control, taking your spirit/soul under control, taking your emotions, feelings and actions under control. It encompasses knowing what is good and making it part of a life style while seeking true knowledge and true understanding of the universe.

To achieve perfect health one must be guided to the doorstep of knowledge, but the guide cannot actually walk through the door with you for the guide is already on the other side. Only you, the person seeking perfect health, can enter and go through the door for perfect health is individually achieved with knowledge and understanding. Attaining perfect health is a choice and a commitment one must make and work on to achieve. No one can achieve perfect health for others; it is an individual decision the individual has to desire and an individual experience.

It is crucial that knowledge and understanding from the Creator is made available to all, but achieved individually. Knowledge and understanding represent the Creator; whoever desires knowledge and understanding must also desire the

Creator. Only when we realize this and enter through the door can we eventually reach perfect health.

Perfect health comes from the knowledge of right and wrong. The most difficult part is to take action that is right for the body, the mind and the soul at all times without fail not only for ourself, but for others, too. This task may seem illusive and unachievable in our practical world but it is possible if we truly meet the Creator and enter through the door without reservation. On the other side of that door is perfect health.

Karma: the supreme law.

We know that the cosmos is ruled by laws. The law of cause and effect allows that where there is an action, there must be a reaction somewhere as the direct result of that action. This same law governs and processes all thoughts, words, and deeds in the universe. We call this law karma. According to the law of karma, all our thoughts, feelings and intentions are given life when manifest. As we execute them, they bear fruit as a consequence. The fruit of our actions, whether good or bad, is be retained and nourished until harvest time. It is as if the universe processes not only our bodies, but everything that we do in life as well.

It is reasonable then, that if all the processes of thought, emotion, and our bodies are interrelated and alive, then there is nothing dead and the whole universe is nothing but the outward reflection of our mind; whatever our actions, deeds, thoughts, and intentions might be, we are the direct beneficiaries of them, both individually and collectively. Since all human actions take place within the universe and it is also known that nothing can escape the universe, we, as individuals living here share everyone else's mental thoughts and actions in the jungle of our collective minds. This means that an innocent thought executed in Africa will become part of the universal mind jungle and ultimately bear fruit on another continent.

Let's take the example of our aura that changes colors leading to unique meanings in interpretation depending of our mental, physical and emotional states and intentions. That alone is a proof that things are being recorded on a continual basis. Another example of this can be seen on our two palms for it is known that the lines in the two palms of our hands are records of our past, our present, and our likely future if we stay on the same course we are on with the same mentality and with the same actions as in the present. The lines and structure of our feet can also tell our lives.

The bottom line is that everything that we do in the universe is recorded and as we are the senders of all things recorded, we are also the receiver of all of those things. Hence, they can either make us happy and healthy or unhappy and unhealthy.

Since it is now fair to say we understand that all that we are or do today is the result of our own past causes, (for we are, in fact, the net result of our own past thoughts and actions), it follows that all that we do, and all that is done to us, happens because it must as the effect of past cause. What is happening in the universe this minute is exactly what should happen because the universe is the direct net result of our individual and collective karmas combined.

Karma does not punish; it only adjusts energy in the universe by following the basic law of cause and effect, also known as "as you sow, so shall you reap." Karma is the law of laws and knows no compromise. We receive retribution by our sins, but not for them. Karma in itself is neither good nor bad but a neutral principle that governs energy and motion of thoughts, words and deeds.

In discussing karma, it is difficult not to also mention fate and destiny because, in my opinion, they are all three the same thing, though explained in different ways. Fate and destiny would not hold if the existence of karma was not a fact. The two are the consequences that follow karma, making karma always inevitably consistent. "Fate" invokes the idea that there is something beyond mankind's reach that governs our life and decrees something will happen to us in a way that is unstoppable for it is out of our control. "Destiny" is what we will live to become as everything that we do at any given time was predetermined and ordered to be so. In sum, both fate and destiny are exactly what karma represents; namely, that whatever action we commit in the course of our life, we will receive back exactly that which we have caused to ourselves, to others and to the universe and it will happen inevitably without the possibility of interference or modification.

Karma, fate and destiny are similar in their effects. Their only difference is that karma takes ground from man's actions while the other two derive from a divine or mysterious source. We don't know if fate and destiny are linked to our own past lives as the law remains supreme and withstands time and space.

Karma holds that any action committed by us in this universe will automatically be stored or recorded within the universe as neutral energy until a certain time when it reaches maturity at which time that same energy will travel back to the sender of the initial action. Karma transforms into fate and destiny when the neutral energy makes its way back to the sender. One has a positive societal connotation as destiny is used to refer to something positive as in, "It was his/her destiny to become president or to achieve this goal" and the other a to something negative as in, "It was his/her fate to have the accident or die at a early age in a brush fire." But, at the end of the day, does it matter when we've been given the freedom to choose?

Let's look at the concepts of chance, luck and coincidence. They are all governed by karma as everything comes back to the sender by creating a series of interconnected and inter-related events (effect) leading back in origin to the prior neutral energy of the sender (cause). Karma determines forever what will happen to an individual every next second as karma is the law that ensures all energy sent by anybody and everybody is balanced through the laws of the universe, guaranteeing that all energy unfolds to keep the universe balanced. Human beings are still left with the free choice to independently and freely choose the way they want to live, how they want to act and what they want to think. We are the only ones who decide whether we go to the left or the right, stop or keep moving.

Karma follows along with us as we go about our day, so it follows that we can change our karma from good to bad or from bad to good when we change the way we behave and act toward other people, ourself and the universe. Karma indeed changes when we change our behaviors, thoughts and intentions. The most profound change to our advantage occurs when we repent by acting in a new spirit and begin doing good deeds for others with love and without expectation of any reward; the cause and effect may end there.

The duality in the universe.

We owe our freedom of action to the fact that everything in the universe is in duality. Death and life, left and right, low and high, east and west, positive and negative come in duality form. Living in this universe, we are exposed to that duality and we have everything and their opposites. Everything in our life involves a choice and there are good choices and bad choices. We have been given the full autonomy of action and it is assumed that we are responsible for our acts, whether good or bad. Each choice we make creates a consequential pattern in the universe. Positive always reaps positive and negative will reap negative. That is what we call the supreme law, which is karma.

If positive brings back positive and negative gives back negative, and assuming we desire positive experiences, it will be wise to conclude that there is a need for everyone to love one another unconditionally and to do for anyone what we would love for them to do for us. To love everyone is not an easy task. It takes a lot of knowledge and understanding of who we are as a person and what we represent to the universe. We must first love ourselves, and later project that love within us onto everyone. It is said that if you want to love, you have to understand and if you want to understand you have to know God and to know God is to love God just as to love God is to feel his love for you. Once we understand, we learn to accept what is, whatever it is, and not wish it to be otherwise.

Human beings, owners of their destiny.

As stated here many times, the universe works through laws. It is believed that everything we do in life from the day we become conscious of right and wrong is recorded in some invisible place as well as in our memories, whether conscious or subconscious. Shortly after birth, we became responsible for drawing our life's destiny. Our thoughts and actions shape our destiny. If we want to be healthy we must practice a way of life that will guaranty our well being.

Daily life shows us that we must actively shape our destiny. Whatever we decide to make of it is our choice. In some ways, we remain responsible even when we are forced to make certain choices under duress or when we are committed to them because of limitations in our knowledge and understanding. In karma's view, nothing is excusable as good or bad actions; both will always be rewarded to the fullest without discrimination or distinction. If we allow ourselves to fall or experience our lower instincts during difficult times, we must act to overcome those instincts in the future, bearing in mind that we are being watched and everything is being recorded.

Because we live in a world where everyone has to literally take matters into their own hands, we are facing an invisible but very real war of minds and thoughts on a daily basis. Everyday we are confronting everybody else's mind and everybody else's thoughts for recognition of stature, riches, respect, love, justice or peace. As we try to impose ourself or to be recognized in any avenue in life, we encounter other people's minds and thoughts also aiming for that same objective. Thus the battle of the minds and thoughts begins and whoever remains focus and strong-minded coupled with perseverance ends up over-achieving.

In a world of competition and where there is an almost total absence of care or tolerance for others, in a world where corruption is found at almost all levels of social classes, love for our neighbor becomes almost nonexistent. In a world where manipulation and confusion tend to be the principal tool to promote the pursuit of personal interest centered on the idea of unconnectedness and the fear of not being successful in life, a lot of people tend to compromise with their very principles and standards of morality simply to make money. Filled with fear that they will be the last in the rat race, many are in this world to win at all costs. They don't worry about the direct or indirect consequences of their own actions upon others or themselves. For the sake of being first, corruption, back stabbing, cheating, lying, manipulating data, committing murder and other violent crimes, become a part of life and whoever excels in these games will surely win the race in a material world. But they truly end up the real loser after all.

It is understandable that the pressure of life itself and the burdens that comes with it all too often will affect and change good to bad, love to hate, altruism to selfishness but at the end of the day we are still responsible for our lives. We are still owners of our destiny because we remain responsible for our choices and actions even if they are not plausible or healthy. Some extreme circumstances may give a sense of legitimacy to our bad actions and bad deeds because of the reasons behind them so that the ends justify the means, but nonetheless the rules do not change. We are what we do and the world is who we are as a people. As it was once said, if we want a better world we should look at ourselves in the mirror and make a change.

Understanding the world.

The world is composed of all kinds of theories, beliefs, cultures, traditions, discoveries, inventions and ideas. Every generation tends to have its own conception of things, tends to author its own explanation of how this and that came to exist. At some point, what one generation perceived and understood as true may appear contradictory to the previous or to the subsequent generations. In sum, evolution has been a compilation of contradiction after contradiction as our views, needs and understandings change from.

We are all hostages in the world of beliefs. Had we been born in a different era, country, or culture, lived in a different neighborhood or received our education in a different school; many of our beliefs may have been different than what they are. It is shocking to realize that many of us almost reach adulthood with false beliefs and false understandings even about the most crucial matters. This realization only comes to each individual when we become interested in discovering the truth and seeking an understanding of the world. We then come to understand that every society has had stories, beliefs, and traditions and provided incentives for the masses to accept them as true, whether or not they were and marginalized or persecuted dissenters as dangerous.

In general, humans can be labeled as purpose-driven creatures that act to promote their own interest and satisfy their own desires and wishes without necessarily taking in account the damages inflicted thereby on their surroundings. Understanding this, we should know that our lives and beliefs reflect the limitations imposed on us by our history, culture, race, class, and gender and, of course our personal circumstances. The world as we see it is nothing more than the product of our beliefs and prejudices which would appear to be only a partial knowledge of our real nature.

It is undeniable that we always learn from people who learned from other people be they teachers, preachers, spiritual leaders, scientists, sages, parents etc. Therefore, our lives and the success of our present intellectual or spiritual efforts are greatly influenced by the beliefs and theories we inherit from the others as well as from the past. We do not gain knowledge with an unbiased, open mind; we will be forever limited to partial and distorted perspectives and understanding, knowing that our judgments and conclusions could be no more accurate than the background theories and beliefs on which we relied on upon to draw our own.

Having understood how our preexisting theories and beliefs strongly influence our understanding of the world, it should humble us while we seek the true truth with no prejudices or we may all be hostages and victims of those prejudices. This is not to assume that everything we know or hear is misleading, but it's wise to apply caution and check the reliability of a belief before embracing it.

Universal relativity of our perceptions and actions.

Another aspect of the universal relativity in all things including people in general can be seen in the way each one of us thinks, perceives life and lives our life. We all live life within the limits of our understanding and our philosophy of society and the universe. The way we behave, the way we interact with others, the way we treat ourselves and our character, all depend on our understanding of the world. Our actions toward ourselves and toward the world are guided by what we know and what we believe to be true. Our actions are always relative to what we know, what we have experienced, and what we believe. Who I am, is how I act. What I know, is truly how I treat my body, my mind and my soul. Who I am, is based on the values I have in life. My predisposition to loving everyone and considering them as equals and forgivable is based on my beliefs, my inner character and my overall understanding of the universe. Importantly, the society we live in will have an impact whether we treat others and ourselves positively or negatively since we owe what we know primarily to it.

But even though we learn mostly from society, there usually comes a time when we begin to become critical and earnestly question certain ways of life society offers and accepts. Society provides positive and negative teachings at the same time. It's up to us to learn to distinguish them and this exercise depends on our inner character and who we decide to become.

On a spiritual level the existence of various cultures and beliefs that exist and have existed mandate us to go within ourselves if we want to find the truth and the true understanding of the world without being prejudicial to others or blame others. We need to understand ourselves first before attempting to understand others or the world in general. We would have to understand our own mind, our own thoughts, our own emotions and our own purpose if we are to see the world with our true pure selves and make any of our actions our own rather than those influenced or inherited.

Understanding yourself and people around you.

To understand yourself, consider yourself at some point in life before awakening, a victim of history and society, causing you to have acted toward yourself and others with prejudices or indifference yet without any guilt because you were limited in knowledge and understanding.

For the next paragraphs I will be using the first person to induce ownership and so that it may be engaging to the reader as having a personal basis.

To understand myself I have to first admit that I'm insane, that I was insane. I had to admit the insanity within me, the insanity that controlled my mind and thoughts. Then I noticed that there were different voices inside me that were triggered anytime I wanted to make a decision or give my opinion on a given subject. One voice would say this, the other would say that and then possibly, a third would say, "Instead of this or that, just do this over here." I realized that I needed to pull all those voices within me together to form one coherent voice so that whatever action I would undertake would be a full representation of me, but not from so many unknown "Me's" inside me. Truly, all that I'd known or learned from society always determined my reactions, whether it was the appropriate or inappropriate action taken, depending on how efficiently society and my 'teachers' taught me. There are actions in our life that we would have not taken if it were not because of some outside influence or limits in understanding preventing us from acting otherwise rather than buying into the influence. Our morals reflect how intensely and extensively our surroundings affect our behaviors.

To achieve my goal of harnessing these various voices within me, I had to practice self control over whatever actions, thoughts and deeds I would do by being mindful at all times with the hope in getting my true self to blossom outwardly. It seemed to me that constant mindfulness would immediately transform me and everything I'd do making my actions come directly from within that authentic person. That way my "Yes" would be Yes and my "No" would be No.

I would also have to cultivate positive thinking at all times by refraining from entertaining bad thoughts, bad ideas, bad wishes, bad desires and bad words. I needed to constantly detect any bad thoughts either destined to myself or to others instinctively before I acted and eradicate them. To achieve this goal, I had to be willing to conscientiously accept the bad as bad and the good as good without trying to distort them. Meaning no more self-justification for bad actions regardless of motives or ends.

Negativity had to be understood as bad if it was bad to start with even if the consequential result may have appeared positive or advantageous to me. The test I used to distinguish between good and bad was simple: did I treat others the same way I wanted them to treat me? In that way I refrained from doing to others what I didn't want them to do to me.

I had to acknowledge all my emotions and label them as positive or negative, bad or good and work on eliminating the negative or bad ones one by one. It is known that emotions such as anger, deceit, hatred, jealousy, fear, pride, lust, greed, rage, retaliation, vengeance, malice, confusion can be classified as negative emotions. They are negative emotions because they have a negative impact on our health and affect people around us negatively, too. It is important to know that when it comes to emotional behavior and reactions, we all fall short at some point in time until we decide to control these. I was told that these negative emotions came from my untamed mind, for it was still selfish as I viewed myself as the center of the world. That mind has been an innocent victim of its surroundings and exposure to society's negativity.

Once I understood this part of me and became aware of where I had fallen short, it was easier to understand people around me when they acted or behaved badly. Having exposed myself to my own limitations and prejudices and having become aware of how difficult it is to be free, humbled me when dealing with others.

Self control, mindfulness and understanding of other people's behaviors and actions are required to stay above any emotional breakdown and negative reactions. When the art of detecting and classifying emotions within oneself was cultivated and dealt with, interactions with others became free from judgment and imparted the ability to understand. Understanding and a self-explanation of how and why I acted a certain way was beneficial and an honest guide to understanding and explaining the acts of others. Through understanding, I became free from self-condemnation and simultaneously stopped judging others. Understanding myself was the key to understanding the world. The world may not be perfect but once we know our true self and truly become responsible for our own actions, it makes a great difference. Only when we know ourself can we move along on our journey without being a victim of predatory teachings.

The Universality of the Truth

We can only find truth when we search for it. Truth is not given; it has to be strived for. Truth has to be known individually. It cannot simply be taught; we can only be guided to it. We can know and read the truth and we may accept it as truth but until we put our own mind and thought to it and meditate on it, we will never understand it as truth. Meditation, intense thinking, contesting it in a critical way are some ways to uncover the truth.

Truth is universal. It cannot be owned by an individual or a certain group of people. It can be transported to the four corners of the globe and demonstrated and still stand as truth. Anything believed to be true that cannot be taken anywhere else in the universe and still remain true is not to be called truth. It may be a convenient truth or an understanding shared by a group of people but it is not the immutable truth.

The truth is not man made; we did not invent the truth and it cannot be manipulated. It has existed prior to humans and we begin to discover it when trying to understand some aspects or mysterious facts of the universe. I can find it, you can find it; anybody anywhere in the universe would be able to find it as it is the reality that exists in the universe. It is not subjective. It is either true everywhere or it's not true at all. Even the smartest, slyest person on earth cannot change or transform the truth to fit their desires and intentions. They can try to hide the truth from us or try to corrupt it as they wish but they cannot stop anyone from discovering the truth for themselves because the truth remains undisturbed and unchanged in the universe.

Whatever that was true in the beginning of time about the universe remains true today and will forever remain true. There is no expiration date on the truth. Truth can be applied every time, everywhere at any given time by anyone who knows it.

Everything our universe provides is eternal truth. Anything found or discovered about the universe is true. Anything man made has failed when tested on a universal level. Any truth that mankind has created is a tinted truth imposed on us, which is subjective and coined to suit someone's intentions and desires, a truth invented to mislead us or to dominate us by feeding us what is not fully true.

Any 'truth' that cannot survive the universality test may not be grounded in truth. Rather, it is the product of pure imagination, invented to draw attention to something or away from something or to make some belief exceptional in the eyes of people.

The truth is independent of human involvement. It does not need to be believed in order to exist. It exists whether we choose to believe or not. It simply exists as the truth. Believe or not, it is there. That the sun rises in the east and goes down in the west is true and remains true even if we choose not to acknowledge or believe it. Someone might choose to call that rounded yellow ball up there something other than the sun, but it does not change the truth: that yellow ball rises up in the same place every morning and rests at the opposite side in the evening only to rise right back in the next morning. The truth remains and is universally true. On this note for the record, we should know that it is earth that turns around the sun even though the sun does turn around at some point at its own pace; earth is the one turning around it. Earth rotates around the sun making it seem like the sun rises and goes down when actually its earth spinning around it in circle.

Quest for the truth and its difficulties.

Society, groups of people, tribes and families were created to fill our need for stability, security, reproducing and, most importantly, as a means of control over us and our actions. People join in union to combine their strengths and better protect themselves, creating their own group identity. For any group, family or society to work properly and to better respond to societal needs, they must be organized. Organization requires rules. Boundaries must be drawn. Everyone in the group has to respect those rules and boundaries or pay the consequences for disobeying them. Ethical and moral values have to be put in place and taught to everyone at the group level to ensure harmony between people, their families, and friends. This way of life developed and was passed down from generation to generation with little or changes made to reflect society's changing needs.

If we assume that cultures, beliefs and traditions develop alongside human history as security to safeguard mankind, there is no doubt that as in times past, some would attempt to take advantage of our culture, our beliefs and traditions to better dominate us. It was customary that if the goal was to destroy a tribe or any group of organized people, one sure way was to interfere with their cultural values and belief systems. It is not surprising that after war, the losing side was forced to give up their own identity as a people and embrace the victor's cultures, beliefs and traditions or else be killed.

I won't insist that our cultures, our beliefs and our traditions are being infiltrated by evil-minded people bent on disorganizing us and leading the world astray according to their plan; however, the bottom line is that no culture in our world has remained uncontaminated from the wishes and desires of some. Before enlightenment, we are selfishly driven by our wishes and desires causing our positions or views to change accordingly. Perhaps we have a constant desire to be right and dominate others at any cost. Nonetheless, we are each charged with the judgment to choose either to be realistic or to stick to the customary belief that if a belief or tradition has survived through time and generations, it must necessarily be true. But if it's a popular belief, must it have a legitimate basis in truth?

The truth is that no culture, belief or tradition deserves to be fully and blindly followed and accepted in all its aspects as our foundation in truth as a guide to deal with others or ourself. The task is on each individual to do our personal due diligence to find the true truth and the true understanding.

In our quest for the truth, it is necessary to consider that no culture, no belief or tradition holds the true truth or is superior to any other and that every culture, belief and tradition in the world might actually have the potential to hold the true truth. We can start by having no belief at all and remain open-minded about everything around us then let the truth impact us as we discover it. Seeking the truth with no set of beliefs is one way to avoid a prejudice that could possibly prevent us from looking everywhere and considering everything.

It may appear a difficult and challenging task to blank our mind from what society, our own culture and beliefs have taught us along the years but it's a road that we must be willing to take if we are to find the answer to our questions. Consciously questioning everything, starting fresh, and considering all possibilities will lead one to the truth. If we hold on to particular belief or culture, we will then compare new beliefs and cultures to those as a measure of credibility. Our goal here is not to find what may make sense or what fits our conception of how things should be, but rather to discover what transcends time and space and remains forever universally true. Because we can only think or perceive things as good or bad by how they compare to what we know, we will be better off leaving all that we already know behind and forget all that we already believe. Then, we will be one step closer to finding the truth.

Truth is only found by the strong-minded people.

The truth cannot be found by a weak-minded person. The search for the truth requires perseverance, determination and a lot of patience, calmness and discipline. It starts by not accepting everything you hear around you in society. If you are quick to give up searching you will never find the truth. The truth is for those of you who dare to question things around you. It takes a lot of curiosity and a lack of interest in what people think about you because once you start looking for the truth, you will drastically change the way you used to do things either with your family or friends or your surroundings and you may even start questioning your mental state.

You stop blindly following others as you now try to understand by asking questions to elders who are reluctant to give you the right answers. One major key in searching for the truth is to practice the art of listening and remaining silent and humble at all times. Keep in mind that people before you have found the truth. So, what you do is meditate on what they have said on all the subjects about the universe and life in general until you fully understand them and can explain them; then you apply them to your inner spirit and start making their connections, one after another, like a chain of truths for one truth leads to another and so on as you keep searching until you discover how the universe works, how each living thing and the entire universe works together, how you function and what you're made of and, most importantly, how all things in the universe are connected and inter-related leading to one source.

Once you realize the unity of all things, you begin to digest all this new knowledge and understanding into your mind and into your soul. Eventually, it will show in your character, in the way you treat yourselves and others. You might soon become a new person with a full understanding of the universe and a full understanding of yourselves and others. The complexity and beauty in each creation and their relation to each other will instill in you a respect for whomever or whatever has created them. Eventually, you will fall in love with the Creator and humbly and totally admit the Creator's supremacy and mightiness over all things. You simply become conscious about your role as being part of the tree of life.

Ultimately, we would care for his creation when we become aware of how the Creator values all living being in the universe by unselfishly protecting, teaching, healing and nurturing it with unconditional love and respect. This ultimate truth is beyond religion, culture, belief and tradition.

It is a fact that as you grow in knowledge and understanding, your mind and soul also grow relatively. Your soul and your mind mature as you discover the truths that come to you one after another. The awakening of your soul and mind take a spiritual dimension as the more you know and understand the more conscious and spiritual you become.

Universal equality of mankind

Human beings are equal. No human life is worth more than another. We all face the same fate in the universe. As we are built the same way from the same Creator, we also share the same destiny. There is no stupid or intelligent human being; we all have flaws. We all have the same basic needs for food, water and a place to sleep. We all entered into the physical world, naked and we will leave the physical world. We have the same mental and spiritual potential and capabilities. The universe allows us all the same opportunities, the same natural laws, the same privileges and above all the same consideration without discrimination.

Life and death are equally shared. Each thing and its opposite dwell in all of us. No one escapes the duality of feelings and emotions such as joy, happiness, sadness, love, hatred, anger, deceit, jealousy, peace, greed, fear, envy and pride, etc. Within us all dwell the good and the bad side by side, the humble and the ego, the wise and the foolish etc.

Knowledge and understanding are equally given and equally available to everyone.

There is no good, there is no bad; everything is perfectly well balanced and equally shared.

The universe neither discriminates, nor loves nor hates. When it rains, it's for everyone. The sun shines for everyone. Moonlight is for everyone to enjoy and the air is abundantly accessible to anybody. Everything from the universe and in the universe is freely given and accessible without conditions.

If there we are experiencing a problem we need to look at ourselves through the mirror and make a change if we want a better tomorrow for ourselves and our offspring's. That's how we make place for wisdom.

God bless.

BIBLIOGRAPHY

- Stefan Chmelik (1999) Chinese herbal secrets (the key to total health)
- Denise Whichello Brown & Sandra White (2001) Alternative Health Therapies (the complete guide to Aromatherapy, Massage and reflexology).
- Barron'st (2nd edition 2004) Anatomy and Physiology (the easy way)
- Paula R. Hartz (1993) Taoism (world Religion)
- Theresa Cheung (2006) The elements encyclopedia of the psychic world (the Ultimate a-z of spirits, mysteries and the paranormal)
- Satguru Sivaya Subramuniyaswami (1993) Dancing with Siva (Hinduism's contemporary catechism)
- Michael Philips (2008) The Undercover philosopher

- Osho (2004) Buddha (his life & teachings)
- Christmas Humphreys (1962) Zen- a way of life
- The Quran
- The Bible
- Divine source (help from the spirits)

www.ingramcontent.com/pod-product-compliance
Lightning Source LLC
Chambersburg PA
CBHW021410290426
44108CB00010B/474